Palm Springs
Travel Guide

Quick Trips Series

No part of this publication may be reproduced, stored in a retrieval system, or transmitted, in any form or by any means without the prior written permission of the publisher, nor be otherwise circulated in any form of binding or cover other than that in which it is published and without similar condition being imposed on the subsequent purchaser. If there are any errors or omissions in copyright acknowledgements the publisher will be pleased to insert the appropriate acknowledgement in any subsequent printing of this publication. Although we have taken all reasonable care in researching this book we make no warranty about the accuracy or completeness of its content and disclaim all liability arising from its use.

Copyright © 2016, Astute Press
All Rights Reserved.

Table of Contents

PALM SPRINGS — 6
- CUSTOMS & CULTURE 9
- GEOGRAPHY 12
- WEATHER & BEST TIME TO VISIT 15

SIGHTS & ACTIVITIES: WHAT TO SEE & DO — 17
- JOSHUA TREE NATIONAL PARK 17
- PALM SPRINGS AERIAL TRAMWAY 21
- PALM SPRINGS AIR MUSEUM 24
- AGUA CALIENTE CULTURAL MUSEUM 26
- HIKING 29
- GENERAL PATTON MEMORIAL MUSEUM 30
- LA QUINTA 32
- PALM DESERT 34
- LAKE ARROWHEAD VILLAGE 36
- SOAK CITY WATER PARK 37

BUDGET TIPS — 40
- ACCOMMODATION 40

  The Curve 40
  Caliente Tropics Hotel 41
  Alcazar Palm Springs 41
  Aqua Soleil 42
  Hotel Zoso 43
◉ **PLACES TO EAT** **44**
  Miro's 44
  Copley's on Palm Canyon 45
  Tropicale 45
  Elmer's Restaurant 46
  Thai Smile 47
◉ **SHOPPING** **48**
  VillageFest 48
  Estate Sale Company 49
  Saks Fifth Avenue 49
  Crystal Fantasy 50
  Tinder Box 51

KNOW BEFORE YOU GO   52

◉ ENTRY REQUIREMENTS 52
◉ HEALTH INSURANCE 53
◉ TRAVELING WITH PETS 54
◉ AIRPORTS 56
◉ AIRLINES 60
◉ HUBS 63
◉ SEAPORTS 65
◉ MONEY MATTERS 67
◉ CURRENCY 67
◉ BANKING/ATMS 67
◉ CREDIT CARDS 68
◉ TOURIST TAX 69

- Sales Tax 70
- Tipping 71
- Connectivity 72
- Mobile Phones 72
- Dialing Code 74
- Emergency Numbers 74
- General Information 74
- Public Holidays 74
- Time Zones 75
- Daylight Savings Time 77
- School Holidays 77
- Trading Hours 78
- Driving 78
- Drinking 80
- Smoking 81
- Electricity 82
- Food & Drink 83
- American Sports 85
- Useful Websites 87

PALM SPRINGS TRAVEL GUIDE

Palm Springs

Located about one hundred miles east of Los Angeles is the inland resort city of Palm Springs, California. Despite its desert location, the city became popular in the mid-20th century when it started to attract Hollywood celebrities. Over the years, Palm Springs has grown into a premier resort attracting all with its year-round sunny weather, golf courses and host of cultural attractions.

PALM SPRINGS TRAVEL GUIDE

With its stunning mountains, mid-twentieth century architecture, scenic trails, and an abundance of entertainment, Palm Springs is a tourist magnet most enjoyable during the non-summer months.

The name of the city probably comes from the native California fan palm although some think that Palm Springs' origin comes from the Spanish term, La Palma de la Mano de Dios, meaning The Palm of God's Hand. The city has also been called Big Palm Springs and Palmetto Springs in the past.

Tourism to the area was started when the Agua Caliente Bathhouse was opened in the 1880s (it is still open and operational). In the next 50 years, nearly a dozen hotels

PALM SPRINGS TRAVEL GUIDE

and two golf courses were opened in the city in a bid to attract tourists.

Palm Springs was an important station for the US Army in the World War II. The 1927 El Mirador Hotel in Palm Springs was bought by the US Government and converted into an army hospital.

Palm Springs' fortune as a resort city grew in the 1950s and 1960s when a number of major Hollywood movie stars chose the city as a quiet and relaxing getaway from Los Angeles.

Major housing projects and shopping centers soon followed. Entertainment and leisure activities were developed with golf tourism being the main focus. From

PALM SPRINGS TRAVEL GUIDE

just 19 courses in the 1960s, Palm Springs now has a staggering 125 golf courses.

Palm Springs has one of the highest percentages of same-sex couples in the United States.

The art and cultural scene is thriving today and ranges from alternative to black-tie galas. Hundreds of restaurants, nightclubs, and bars offer a wide range of entertainment to patrons.

Area attractions range from national parks, scenic hiking trails to celebrity-home tours and art museums.

Accommodation in the city ranges from historic inns and backpacker hostels all the way to ultra-modern 5 star hotels.

PALM SPRINGS TRAVEL GUIDE

From its start as a virtual ghost town, Palm Springs has transformed itself into the vibrant resort city of today.

🌏 Customs & Culture

The cultural calendar of Palm Springs is active throughout the year. The most prominent annual event is the Palm Springs International Film Festival in January - http://www.psfilmfest.org/index.aspx. The 10-day film festival, one of the most popular in the USA, attracts some of the biggest names of the film industry. Over 200 films from nearly 60 countries are screened in the festival that includes a black-tie awards gala.

Other annual film festivals include the Festival of Native Film and Culture, the International Festival of Short Films,

PALM SPRINGS TRAVEL GUIDE

the Film Noir Festival, and the Cinema Diverse Gay and Lesbian Films.

Theater lovers can head to the Historic Plaza Theater that hosts the famous Fabulous Palm Springs Follies show - http://www.psfollies.com/.

February has the Tour de Palm Springs cycling event - http://www.tourdepalmsprings.com attracting hundreds of cyclists for its 25, 55, and 100 mile races. The Modernism Week - http://www.modernismweek.com/ in mid-February celebrates the mid century architecture and design in Palm Springs through numerous tours, lectures, movies, and exhibitions.

In April there is the popular White Party - http://whiteparty.org/ catering to the LGBT community and

PALM SPRINGS TRAVEL GUIDE

attracting patrons and supporters from every community. Another major LGBT event is the Dinah Shore Weekend - http://thedinah.com in March, considered the largest lesbian festival in the world. The 5-day event features numerous live concerts, parties, comedy shows, games, and night entertainment.

Winter months see a number of parades in Palm Springs, the most popular being the Homecoming Parade, the Veterans Day Parade, and the Palm Springs Festival of Lights Parade. Car lovers can head to the American Heat Bike Show or the Exotic Car Show and Auction. The Christmas Tree Lighting at the iconic Palm Springs Aerial Tramway is also a major crowd puller.

Sports lovers can choose from a number of events in the city. Baseball and tennis is popular in the city (the BNP

PALM SPRINGS TRAVEL GUIDE

Paribas Tennis Tournament is one of the premier tennis tournaments in the world); but the one sport that demands special mention is golf. With over a hundred courses having over 2000 holes, Palm Springs is the haven for golf lovers. Such is the popularity of golf in this city that more than 2.1 million gallons of water is spent to keep the courses fit for play, and that too, in a desert city!

The first to come up was the O'Donnell Golf Club in 1927 followed closely by the El Mirador Hotel Golf Course. The city saw its first 18-hole course after the World War II. In 2001, the 100th course was opened in Palm Springs. Today the city is home to the PGA Humana Challenge, the LPGA Kraft Nabisco Championship, and the Desert Dunes Classic. Amateurs and professionals can choose from a number of courses of varying difficulties. Details of golf courses in Palm Springs along with the tee times and course rates can be found at -

http://palmsprings.com/golf.html and

http://www.psgolfcourses.com/.

🌐 Geography

Palm Springs is located about 100 miles east of Los Angeles and about 120 miles northeast of San Diego. Being just a two-hour drive away from these two cities, Palm Springs is well connected by road. Attracting over 1.6 million tourists from all corners of the globe, the city also has very good flight connectivity.

Palm Springs is served by the Palm Springs International Airport (IATA: PSP) that has regular direct connections to many major US and Canadian cities. It is located just 2 miles east of the city downtown. Other than the regular commercial passenger flights, the airport - which attracts

PALM SPRINGS TRAVEL GUIDE

many business travelers – is served by many private aircraft charter companies including Jetset Charter - http://www.jscharter.com/, Desertjet - http://www.desertjet.com/, and Air Royale International - http://airroyale.com/.

The neighboring airport in Los Angeles - LA/Ontario International Airport - http://www.lawa.org/ has more connections globally as well as in the US. Located just 70 miles from Palm Springs and connected by a host of private and public transportation facilities, the airport is often the preferred choice for those who are flying across the Pacific.

Palm Springs is connected by rail through Amtrak - http://www.amtrak.com/servlet/ContentServer?c=am2Station&pagename=am%2Fam2Station%2FStation_Page&p=

PALM SPRINGS TRAVEL GUIDE

<u>1237405732508&cid=1229726270390</u>. The station is located at North Indian Canyon Drive to the south of the I-10 Highway. There are multiple connections every week to Los Angeles, Bay Area, and Sacramento in California. Weekly connections are also available with Arizona. However, it is to be kept in mind that there is no station building in Palm Springs. There is not even any washroom, platform, or payphone. Without even a rental car company in the station area, one must first arrange for a pickup before deciding to take the train to Palm Springs.

For those deciding to drive, the city is easily accessible through the I-10 East highway. Keep following the route/signs to Phoenix from Los Angeles. A number of bus services, including Greyhound - <u>http://www.greyhound.com/</u> connect Palm Springs to other American cities.

PALM SPRINGS TRAVEL GUIDE

Once in the city, the best and the easiest way to move around is with a private vehicle. The city has many car rental companies to choose from; from the economic sedans to the luxury limousines. Public transport is available in the form of buses - http://www.sunline.org/home/index.asp. With a fare of $1 for a one-way adult ticket, one can see most part of the city and its attractions. Taxis are readily available with the meter charging $2.80 per mile. For the health conscious and eco-friendly visitors, cycling is an option as most of Palm Springs is flat with cycle-friendly paths.

Weather & Best Time to Visit

With nearly 350 days of sunshine and less than 5 inches of annual rainfall, Palm Springs has a hot and dry climate. Summer temperatures between May and September can

PALM SPRINGS TRAVEL GUIDE

reach a high of about 100 degrees Fahrenheit and a low of around 80 degrees; the average hovers around 75 degrees. Winter months between November and March can see the temperature fall to around 40 degrees Fahrenheit and the highs between 70 and 80 degrees. December, January and February have some short infrequent showers. The year round sunny weather makes it an ideal tourist destination throughout the year but Palm Springs is best avoided in the peak of summer (June to September) when it may get too hot for many visitors. January to March is the high season.

PALM SPRINGS TRAVEL GUIDE

Sights & Activities: What to See & Do
🌏 Joshua Tree National Park

http://www.nps.gov/jotr/index.htm

PALM SPRINGS TRAVEL GUIDE

Spanning over 1235 sq miles, the Joshua Tree National Park, is a US National Park and a major tourist landmark in the state of California. The region was originally a US National Monument (since 1936) before it was designated a National Park in 1994. The park is named after the unique Joshua tree, which itself was named by the Mormons in the mid 19th century who felt that the tree looked the hands of the Biblical Joshua raised towards the sky. 'The Joshua Tree', a best-selling album by U2 in 1987, featuring a photo of the park with its unique flora on its cover, raised the profile and interest of the Park amongst the public manifold.

The landscape of the park is dominated by two deserts, the Colorado Desert and the Mojave Desert. These 2 deserts are at 2 different elevations prompting 2 very distinct ecosystems within the boundary of the park. The

PALM SPRINGS TRAVEL GUIDE

Colorado Desert, which is below 3000 feet, is on the eastern side of the park, and has natural gardens, cacti - especially the beautiful teddy-bear cholla cactus, and ocotillo. On a higher elevation is the cooler and moister Mojave Desert. It is the habitat of the famed Joshua tree. Due to the presence of moisture, there are five fan-palm oases in the Mojave Desert and one can also find a number of wildlife. The Mojave Desert is home to some of the most stunning landscapes including the Giant Marbles, the Old Woman Rock, and the North Horror Rock.

Although the park is made up of two deserts and the area apparently seems arid and lifeless, there are a number of desert flora and fauna. Other than the dominant Joshua tree, oak varieties, like the desert scrub, Tucker's, and the Muller's oak are found in the rocky areas. Pinon pine and

PALM SPRINGS TRAVEL GUIDE

the California juniper are also common varieties found in the park. However, a large part of the park area is covered by the invasive cheatgrass – a species that is very prone to wildfires. Other than the usual lizards, snakes, and ground squirrels, the park wildlife includes coyotes, jackrabbits, kangaroo rats, and a few bobcats. At the Barker Dam near the Hidden Valley, one can see Mule Deer and the Desert Bighorn Sheep. Other varieties include the tree frog, red-spotted toad, the roadrunner, golden eagle, the giant desert scorpion and the yucca moth. The park is home to more than 250 species of birds which include the cactus wren, mockingbird, and the quail. Owls and vultures are also commonly sighted.

The park has many facilities for a variety of recreation. There are opportunities for climbing, hiking, camping, birdwatching, as well as stargazing. The park area has 9

PALM SPRINGS TRAVEL GUIDE

campground sites, out of which 3 camping sites are equipped with water and flush-toilets. These sites are Cottonwood Campground, Indian Cove Campground, and Black Rock Campground. The first 2 sites are open for reservations from October until May, while the last one operates on a first-come-first-serve system. There is a fee payable at each of these sites on a per night basis. However, those who are planning to stay overnight should keep in mind that the Joshua Tree National Park is ranked within the top 3 US National Parks with the worst air pollution level.

With its stunning rocky landscape, the Joshua Tree National Park offers many hiking trails, some coming with lookout points. From shorter trails – like the 1 mile trail in Hidden Valley – to much longer ones – like the 35 mile trail in the California Riding and Hiking Trail – one can

PALM SPRINGS TRAVEL GUIDE

choose from a wide variety depending on time, fitness, and location. Some of the longer trails include the Boy Scout (16 miles), Lost Horse Mine (4 miles), Lost Palms Oasis (8 miles), and the Ryan Mountain (3 miles). Unfortunately, some interesting and beautiful sites on some of the trails (including some Native American sites and the Barker Dam) have been closed due to graffiti and vandalism.

For the less adventurous, there is birdwatching and stargazing. The list of birds that have been spotted and can be seen in the Park can be found at the site of the US Geological Survey at http://www.usgs.gov/. Stargazers in California often flock in the park area because of the dark skies and dry air which is ideal for star gazing.

PALM SPRINGS TRAVEL GUIDE

The Park is well connected by road from Palm Springs. Once in the Park, one can use a vehicle to move around; a 4-wheel drive is recommended for the terrain. There are a number of sites that one can visit when in the park for its unique beauty including the Cholla Cactus Garden, Cottonwoods Springs, Barker Dam, and the Hidden Valley.

🌐 Palm Springs Aerial Tramway

1 Tram Way

Palm Springs, CA 992262

Tel: 760 325 1391

http://www.pstramway.com/

Opened in 1963 to connect the Coachella Valley to the top of San Jacinto Peak, the iconic Palm Springs Aerial Tramway is the largest rotating aerial tramway in the

PALM SPRINGS TRAVEL GUIDE

world. One of the major tourist attractions of Palm Springs, this aerial tramway ride not only provides some stunning views of the valley and the mountain, it also cut down the time to reach the top of the mountain from a few hours' hike to a mere 12 minutes.

The ride starts at the Valley Station at Coachella Valley and ends at the Mountain Station, 2596m above sea level. During the course of the ride, the tramcar passes through 5 biomes – life zones with similar flora and fauna – from the Sonoran Desert to the alpine forest. This change in the biomes can see a fall in temperature by nearly 40 degrees Fahrenheit at the mountain top!

During the course of the ride, the floor of tramcars rotates on its axis a full 360 degrees so that the riders can see the view on all sides without moving. Each tramcar-floor

PALM SPRINGS TRAVEL GUIDE

completes 2 full loops during the ride. The tramcars, with a diameter of 5.5m and a passenger capacity of 80 are the largest rotating aerial tramcars in the world. These rotating aerial tramways are just one of the three in the world, the other two being in South Africa and in Switzerland. As there is no other road to the top of the mountain, the tramcars are also used to transport food and water. The underbelly of the tramcars is used to carry water and the passenger cell to transfer food and other utilities, before the attractions open to the public.

Once at the summit, one can go for a hike, walking trails, play in the snow, or even go for a backcountry hike, although the latter needs a permit from the US Forest Service. Free guided nature walks are also available at the summit. For those who want to relax and enjoy the view, there are 2 restaurants – the fine dining Peak's

PALM SPRINGS TRAVEL GUIDE

Restaurant and the Pines Café. There is also a full cocktail bar at the same level – the Lookout Lounge. On a clear day, one can see as far as 200 miles northwards and about 75 miles towards east or west.

Although the prices and hours of operation change depending on the weather and season; usually, between Monday and Friday, the first tram goes up at 10:00 am and the last tram goes up at 8:00 pm. The last tram coming down is at 9:45 pm. Trams leave at least every 30 minutes. On weekends and holidays, the tramcars start at 8:00 am. Pets are not allowed on the tramcars, and children below the age of 16 must be accompanies by an adult of 21 years or older.

Ticket prices for the ride is: Adult - $23.95; Child (3 to 12 years) - $16.95. There is a Ride n Dine Pass available after 4:00 pm which includes a round trip ride and dining in the Pines Café. The Pass costs: Adult - $36; Child – 23.50.

🌐 Palm Springs Air Museum

745 N Gene Autry Trail

Palm Springs, CA 92262

Tel: 760 778 6262

http://palmspringsairmuseum.org/

Located just north east of the Palm Springs International Airport, the Palm Springs Air Museum is one of the premier air force museums having one of the largest collections of flyable World War II aircrafts in the world. This non-profit educational museum has a mission to exhibit and educate visitors on World War II aircrafts and

PALM SPRINGS TRAVEL GUIDE

also to highlight the role of the American fighter pilots in the war.

The aircrafts – many of which have been used in war movies – are displayed in three large hangars in the facility that spans 70000 sq ft. Aircrafts include the Supermarine Spitfire, Bell Cobra Gunship, F-14 Tomcat, B-17 Flying Fortress, F6F Hellcat, F-4 Phantom, and the P-51 Mustang, to name a few. The museum also has a gift shop, theater, research library, simulation center, a ramp, and an airport access for flight demonstrations. The museum is often rented for gala events and private parties.

Pre-arranged group tours are available with guides who are often veteran air force pilots. These 1.5-2 hr tours require at least a 2-week advance notice. A maximum of

PALM SPRINGS TRAVEL GUIDE

15 members are allowed in a group with a free bus driver provided to move from one hangar to another.

The Air Museum is open every day (except Christmas Day, Thanksgiving Day, and Feb 7th) from 10:00 am to 5:00 pm. Entry fee for the museum: Adult - $15. Discounts for children and seniors are available except on Saturdays and holidays. Tickets and tour booking can be done online.

🌐 Agua Caliente Cultural Museum

Village Green Heritage Center

219 S Palm Canyon Drive

Palm Springs CA 92262

Tel: 760 778 1079

http://www.accmuseum.org

PALM SPRINGS TRAVEL GUIDE

Founded in 1991, the Agua Caliente Cultural Museum is a non-profit organization aimed at preserving, interpreting, and providing access to the culture and history of the Cahuilla people, especially the Agua Caliente Band of the Cahuilla Indians. This museum is the first Native American Museum that is a part of the renowned Smithsonian Institution Affiliations Program enabling it to bring quality exhibitions, world class tours, and technical expertise to the natives of the Coachella Valley.

Collections in the museum are focused on the Agua Caliente band although there are artifacts from other Native American tribes as well as from indigenous tribes from different corners of the globe. A popular exhibit is the basket collection from the basket weavers of the tribal communities of the Coachella Valley. This collection of over 400 items has proved to be a great resource to study the comparative changes over the years in techniques and styles of weaving. Other collections include household accessories and tools of ceramics. Buttons, bottles, cans, and china from early habitation sites are also preserved in the museum. With over 50000 objects, the Tahquitz Canyon Archaeological Collection from a village site is one of the largest such collections in the state of California. The museum is presently adding contemporary art and artifacts in its collections. Some of these collections are available by appointment only for researchers and students.

The museum has a number of permanent exhibitions which portray the history and culture of the various indigenous tribes in the Coachella Valley. These exhibitions include archeological materials, arts, crafts,

PALM SPRINGS TRAVEL GUIDE

publications, documents, photographs, and even the audiovisual media. Some of the exhibitions are also available online with the links provided in the museum website. Additional exhibits and photographs are displayed at the Palm Springs City Hall, Palm Springs Visitors Center, the California State University, and the Spa Resort Casino Hotel.

From September through May, the museum is open from Wednesday to Sunday from 10:00 am until 5:00 pm. Between June and August; it is open for the same hours only from Friday to Sunday. It is closed on Thanksgiving, Christmas, and New Year's Day. The museum has free entry.

 Hiking

There is an abundance of hiking trails in Palm Springs. The stunning rocky landscape spotted with alpine wilderness gives the outdoor enthusiast enough opportunities to enjoy the beauty of nature.

One of the most popular and scenic hikes is to the town of Idyllwild - http://www.idyllwild.com/ located in a mile high elevation on the San Jacinto Mountains. The 10-mile picturesque hike starts from the Mountain Station of the aerial tramway and ends at 2 miles from the Idyllwild town center at Humber Park. Other hikes in the Idyllwild region include the Ernie Maxwell Scenic Trail – a flattish relaxing 2-mile hike from Humber Park; and Tahquitz Peak – a 4-hr hike to a neighboring lookout tower with excellent panoramic views.

PALM SPRINGS TRAVEL GUIDE

Other popular hikes that are recommended in Palm Springs include the 2-mile Andreas Canyon Trail Loop (approx 1.5 hrs) along a quiet stream in the native Cahuilla region. The 2-mile Palm Springs Arts Museum Trail (approx 2 hrs) is a steep ascent to a picnic spot with a viewpoint of the whole valley. The 6-mile Araby Trail (4 hrs) is a free trail off the 111 Highway and rises above the scenic Bob Hope Estate.

The 8-mile Murray Hill Trail (6 hrs) is one of the best hikes in Palm Springs for its views of both sides of the valley. The hike ends at a picnic spot on top of the Murray Hill. There are a number of other hiking trails in Palm Springs area, details of which can be found at http://www.blm.gov/ca/st/en/fo/palmsprings/santarosa/trail headsb.html.

PALM SPRINGS TRAVEL GUIDE

🌐 General Patton Memorial Museum

2 Chriaco Summit Road, Chriaco Summit, CA 92201

Tel: 760 227 3483

http://generalpattonmuseum.com

Named after and dedicated to the legendary US Army General George Patton Jr, the General Patton Memorial Museum at the Chiriaco Summit is a non-profit museum dedicated to the various wars the USA was involved in, from the Civil War to the Iraq conflict in the late 20th century.

The museum is about an hour's drive from Palm Springs. The museum is named after General Patton as the site was handpicked by the General for his training lessons. The site was located close to the General's headquarters and was initially chosen to house the history and information about the Desert Training Center, a facility that trained over a million Americans for the World War II. The museum was opened on November 11th (in 1988), General Patton's birthday.

The Museum has a number of Remembrance Walls dedicated to the different wars. The Korean War Remembrance Wall is dedicated to the Korean War (1950-54) veterans and to all those who have been stationed there, to the present date. The Defenders of Freedom Remembrance Wall is dedicated to war veterans from the Gulf War to the present day international conflicts, along with members of the public responder services like the firemen and law enforcers. The World War Walls are dedicated to the veterans of the 2 Wars. The Vietnam Era Service Wall is dedicated to those who served anywhere during the Vietnam War. Tiles or bricks dedicated to the veterans to be placed on the wall can be bought at a donation, details of which are given in the website. Visitors, on the other hand, can buy gifts and apparel from the museum gift store.

The museum is open every day (except Christmas Day and Thanksgiving Day) from 9:30 am to 4:30 pm. Entry fee to the museum is: Adult - $5, Child - $1, Seniors - $4.50.

🌐 La Quinta

Located about 30 minutes southeast of the city of Palm Springs is the desert resort city of La Quinta. La Quinta is surrounded with mountains and has ample opportunities for fine dining and shopping, but with 28 golf courses

PALM SPRINGS TRAVEL GUIDE

within its city limits, it has emerged as one of the premier golfing destinations in the country.

Those driving from Palm Springs have to take the I-10 East Highway and then take the Washington Street or Jefferson Street exit. La Quinta is located a further 5 mile drive southbound. For those not having a vehicle can take the bus; Greyhound - http://www.greyhound.com/ and Amtrack California - http://www.amtrakcalifornia.com/ have connections to the city. Within the city limits, one can see most of downtown – known as Village – on foot. There are a couple of bus routes although cycling is more common. The city also allows the use of golf carts on its streets!

The biggest attraction of the city is, of course the golf courses - http://www.laquintaresort.com/5_golf_courses/.

PALM SPRINGS TRAVEL GUIDE

Not only are there golf courses of varying difficulties, the golf resorts are often equipped with golf stores making La Quinta an ideal place to buy golf accessories. The surrounding landscape is a delight for hikers. The Bear Creek Trail and the trailhead at neighborhood Cove are popular. Those who are looking for a nature getaway within the city can head to the stunning 710-acre Lake Cahuilla Park at the base of the Santa Rosa Mountains. The park is located 6 miles south east of downtown. La Quinta also has a number of other attractions ranging from casinos to tennis and horseback riding clubs. The downtown - http://www.oldtownlaquinta.com/ with its historic ambience, variety of shops, and a range of restaurants and bars, is a popular hangout for locals and visitors alike.

🌍 Palm Desert

Located at the base of the San Jacinto Mountains, the city of Palm Desert is a popular tourist getaway with its stunning golf courses, luxury hotels, spas, and shopping opportunities. The city is about a 2-hr drive from Palm Springs but traffic can be heavy on weekends making the journey time longer. Within the city, one can use the public bus or the free shuttle, but it is, like many other US cities, primarily a car-oriented city.

Other than the golf and tennis opportunities, Palm Desert has a number of attractions for the whole family. The Living Desert Zoo and Gardens - http://www.livingdesert.org/, the Palm Desert Civic Center Park - http://www.cityofpalmdesert.org/Index.aspx?page=183, and the Palm Desert Aquatic Center are aimed to

PALM SPRINGS TRAVEL GUIDE

entertain the whole family. The McCallum Theater - http://www.mccallumtheatre.com/ with its plays and ballets, the Art Museum - http://www.psmuseum.org/palm-desert/, and the Historical Society and Museum - http://www.hspd.org/home.html are also popular with the tourists. One can take a casual stroll in the city streets and enjoy more than 130 public arts that dot the city. For a more organized tour, there are the Elite Land Tours - http://www.elitelandtours.com/, the Big Wheel Tours - http://www.bwbtours.com/, and the Desert Adventure Jeep Tours - http://red-jeep.com/.

The city is a delight for food lovers. Other than the many bars, restaurants, and cafes that are found in all corners of the city, food lovers can take the popular Desert Tasty Tour - http://www.deserttastytours.com/ and enjoy a fun culinary journey of La Quinta.

PALM SPRINGS TRAVEL GUIDE

🌐 Lake Arrowhead Village

Located about 70 miles northwest of Palm Springs, the mountain resort of Lake Arrowhead Village is an extremely popular tourist destination, attracting over 4 million visitors every year. Almost completely supported by tourism, the main attraction is the Lake Arrowhead (formerly called the Little Bear Lake until the Lake Arrowhead Company bought and renamed it). Other than the recreation activities in the Lake, the surrounding areas offer opportunities in hiking, cycling, snow skiing, and backpacking. The city is also a popular venue for concerts and festivals. Lake Arrowhead is home to the largest free Oktoberfest in the USA. It also hosts many car shows, animal shows, and the popular annual Summer Concert Series.

PALM SPRINGS TRAVEL GUIDE

With over 400 hotel guestrooms and over 500 cabins and condos, the city has a wide range of accommodations to choose from. There are many shops and retail stores ranging from the quintessential grocery store to the chic boutique. Sales announcements and coupons for the stores can be found at http://www.thelakearrowheadvillage.com/#!coupons--sales/c1vdk.

Soak City Water Park

1500 S Gene Autrey Trail

Palm Springs, CA 92264

Tel: 760 327 0499

https://www.soakcityps.com/

Reopening in 2014 under a new management, the Soak City Water Park (previously known as Knott's Soak City in

PALM SPRINGS TRAVEL GUIDE

Palm Springs) is 16-acre popular seasonal water park, a perfect outing for the whole family. Adjacent to the pool is an outdoor amusement park. The park has over 20 water-rides and attractions including 13 water slides, a river-tube ride, a big wave pool, and kids' activity and fun zone.

The rides are built with a 1950s theme. The park has a 4-storey tall interactive playhouse called the Kahuna Beach House. Another exciting attraction is the multi-person raft-ride with its 132 ft long tunnel and near 75 ft drop! There is also a snack bar as well as a souvenir store in the premises. The Park is usually open daily from Memorial Day (around mid-March) to Labor Day (early Sep). Tickets and passes can be bought at the gates but are available at a discount if bought in advance online.

PALM SPRINGS TRAVEL GUIDE

PALM SPRINGS TRAVEL GUIDE

Budget Tips

Accommodation

The Curve

333 E Palm Canyon Dr.

Palm Springs, CA 92264

Tel: 760 327 1211

http://www.curvepalmsprings.com

Located close to the Agua Caliente Cultural Museum and about a mile away from the nightlife spot of Palm Springs, The Curve is a 2.5 start hotel with free parking and a 24-hr reception. The hotel has an outdoor pool, a spa, a pool cabana, and a picnic area inside its smoke-free property. There is free Wi-Fi. It has a bar, restaurant and a café. The ensuite rooms have refrigerators, flat TVs, and some come with a balcony. Room rates start from $55.

Caliente Tropics Hotel

411 E Palm Canyon Dr

Palm Springs, CA 92264

Tel: 760 327 1391

http://www.calientetropics.com/

Located close to Palm Springs Air Museum and the Plaza Theatre, the Caliente Tropics Hotel is a 2.5 star property with 90 ensuite air-conditioned rooms. This family friendly hotel has free parking, concierge service, picnic area, outdoor pool, and a travel desk. It has free Wi-Fi. Pets are allowed. There is an onsite restaurant and café. Rooms are fully equipped and come with a safe. The rates start from $55.

PALM SPRINGS TRAVEL GUIDE

Alcazar Palm Springs

622 N Palm Canyon Dr

Palm Springs, CA 92262

Tel: 760 318 9850

http://www.alcazarpalmsprings.com

This tastefully decorated 3-star hotel has 2 types of rooms – the superior mountain-view rooms and the pool-view rooms. It is located close to the Palm Springs Aerial Tramway. It has free parking and Wi-Fi. The hotel has a multilingual staff and concierge services. There is an outdoor pool, spa, patio, and a bar. The 32 ensuite rooms have all modern facilities including a hair dryer. Room rates start from $99 for the poolside facing rooms.

PALM SPRINGS TRAVEL GUIDE

Aqua Soleil

14500 Palm Drive

Desert Hot Springs

Palm Springs, CA 92240

Tel: 760 329 1409

http://www.aquasoleilhotel.com/

The Aqua Soleil Hotel and Mineral Spa is a 3-star property and is located close to the Desert Dunes Golf Club and the Palm Springs Air Museum. This smoke-free property comes with a 24-hr front desk, concierge service, and multilingual staff. . It has free parking and Wi-Fi. The hotel has a pool, a fully-equipped spa, and a massage center. Cribs (infant beds) are not available. The 80 ensuite rooms come with a private patio. Room rates start from $90.

PALM SPRINGS TRAVEL GUIDE

Hotel Zoso

150 S Indian Canyon Dr, Palm Springs, CA 92262

Tel: 760 325 9676

http://www.hotelzoso.com/

Located adjacent to the Plaza Theatre, Hotel Zoso is a 4-star hotel with 163 air-conditioned rooms. The hotel has a 24-hr reception, concierge service, travel desk, bellhop, and multilingual staff. There is free Wi-Fi. The hotel has a souvenir store, poolside bar, spa, designated smoking area, and laundry facility. There is an onsite restaurant. The rates for the elegantly decorated rooms start from $89.

PALM SPRINGS TRAVEL GUIDE

 Places to Eat

Miro's

1555 S Palm Canyon Dr

Palm Springs, CA 92264

Tel: 760 323 5199

http://mirospalmsprings.com

The Miro's serves German and Hungarian cuisine cooked in a home-style manner. The popularity of the restaurant means it is best to reserve a table before going there. The restaurant is only open for dinner from 5:00 pm until late hours every day. Appetizers like cabbage rolls start from $8. Fish and seafood dishes include shrimps and salmon from $28. Main dishes include Rack of Lamb ($37), Crispy Duckling ($32), Mediterranean Chicken ($25), and some other European dishes. It also serves Californian and Italian wine.

Copley's on Palm Canyon

621 N Palm Canyon Dr, Palm Springs, CA 92262

Tel: 760 327 9555

http://www.copleyspalmsprings.com/

Located in a beautiful courtyard amidst a lot of green, the 'Copley's' serves American and contemporary cuisine with a mix of tropical and European flavors.

It is open only for dinner. The appetizer list includes Hawaiian Tacos ($15), and Ravioli ($12). Entrees have grilled salmon ($29), BBQ pork ($32), tofu with vegetables ($22), and Maine lobster ($34).

Tropicale

330 E Amado Road,

Palm Springs, CA 92262

Tel: 760 866 1952

http://thetropicale.com/

Located close to the Spa Resort Casino, the Tropicale serves American cuisine in a warm and friendly ambience. The tables, set up on a patio, create a very romantic and feel-good atmosphere that is coupled with some deliciously cooked dishes. Starters include duck, crab, and a vegetarian dish. Entrees include clams in tomato wine broth, roasted Brussels sprouts, and roasted organic boneless chicken, to name a few. Small plates and sandwiches are also available. The restaurant also serves brunch. It serves a variety of wines and spirits.

Elmer's Restaurant

1030 E Palm Canyon Dr, Palm Springs, CA 92264

Tel: 760 327 8419

http://eatatelmers.com

The Elmer's is a chain of 24 restaurants along the west coast of USA. It opens for breakfast and serves until late hours for dinner.

It has a variety of menus to choose from – core menu, kid's menu, nutritional menu, to-go menu, and healthy choices menu! The restaurant serves popular American cuisine. Breakfast menu has crepes, eggs, bacon, and pancakes. Main dishes (for lunch and dinner) include steak, pot roast, and a variety of sandwiches and burgers.

PALM SPRINGS TRAVEL GUIDE

Thai Smile

100 S Indian Canyon Dr, Palm Springs, CA 92262

Tel: 760 320 5503

http://www.thaismilepalmsprings.com/

This multi-award winning Thai restaurant has a simple elegant décor and excellent food. The restaurant has a wide selection of items to choose from and includes a menu for vegetarians.

There is a special lunch package everyday from 11:00 am to 4:00 pm. Soups start from $4.50 per cup and entrees are priced between $12 and $17. The special Thai curries are priced $11 ($13 for shrimp or duck). Thai desserts that are served include ice cream with bananas ($7.95), and sticky rice with mango slices ($5.95).

 Shopping

VillageFest

http://villagefest.org/

Also known as the Palm Springs Street Fair, the VillageFest is a weekly fair that is set up in downtown Palm Springs every Thursday evening. Popular with the locals and visitors alike, the fair includes a variety of items and exhibits to enjoy and buy. There is a huge array of arts, crafts, entertainment, and of course, food. The fair attracts thousands of visitors who can buy jewelry, local handmade crafts, flowers, and fresh produce from this fair-cum-market. It is usually open from 6:00 pm to 10:00 pm.

Estate Sale Company

4185 E Palm Canyon Dr, Palm Springs, CA 92264

Tel: 760 321 7628

http://www.theestatesaleco.com/

This family owned consignment store stocks and sells a wide variety of items that include fine furniture, estate jewelry, fine art and accessories, outdoor ornamental art, and patio furniture. The Palm Springs Life Magazine voted the store as the Best Consignment Store in Palm Springs. 100000 sq ft of the finest items spread over the whole block makes it one of the must visit shopping places in Palm Springs.

Saks Fifth Avenue

Tahquitz Canyon

Palm Springs, CA

http://www.saksfifthavenue.com/Entry.jsp

This renowned designer department store is for those who are looking for high end clothing for men or women from the established brands. Items include apparel, jewelry, accessories, shoes, and beauty products. The store has a number of famous brands like D&G, Donna Karan, Fendi, Armani, Gucci, Jimmy Choo, Ralph Lauren, and Prada.

Crystal Fantasy

268 N Palm Canyon Dr

Palm Springs, CA 92262

Tel: 760 322 7799

http://www.crystalfantasy.com/

Featuring mineral and crystals from around the world, this

store has earned a reputation for its unique and exquisite craftsmanship. The store doubles up as a spiritual enlightenment center. Perfect place to pick the special gift for the friend and the family and leave with a more positive energy! The store is open from 11:00 am until 7:00 pm with extended hours (close at 9:00 pm) from Thursday to Saturday.

Tinder Box

200 N Palm Canyon Dr

Palm Springs, CA 92262

Tel: 760 325 4041

http://www.tinderboxpalmsprings.com/

Established in 1928, the store sells unique and quality products linked with tobacco and gifts from around the world. The store sells a variety of special edition pipes and lighters, prices of which may go up to $325! It also sells some unique varieties of flavored tobaccos.

Know Before You Go

Entry Requirements

The Visa Waiver Programme (VWP) allows nationals of selected countries to enter the United States for tourism or certain types of business without requiring a visa. This applies to citizens of the UK, Australia, New Zealand, Canada, Chile, Denmark, Belgium, Austria, Latvia, Estonia, Finland, Italy, Hungary, Iceland, France, Germany, Japan, Spain, Portugal, Norway, Sweden, Slovenia, Slovakia, Switzerland, Brunei, Taiwan, South Korea, Luxemburg, Singapore, Liechtenstein, Monaco, Malta, San Marino, Lithuania, Greece, the Netherlands and the Czech Republic. To qualify, you will also need to have a passport with integrated chip, also known as an e-Passport. The e-Passport symbol has to be clearly displayed on the cover of the passport. This secure method of identification will protect and verify the holder in case of identity theft and other breaches of privacy. There are exceptions. Visitors with a criminal record, serious communicable illness or those who were deported or refused entry on a past occasion will not qualify for the Visa Waiver Program and will need to apply for a visa. Holders of a UK passport who have dual citizenship of Iraq, Iran, Sudan, Syria, Somalia, Libya or Yemen (or those who have travelled to the above countries after 2011) will also need to apply for a visa. A requirement of the Visa Waiver Programme is online registration with the Electronic System for Travel Authorisation (ESTA) at least 72 hours before your travels. When entering the United States, you will be able to skip the custom declaration and proceed directly to an Automated Passport Control (APC) kiosk.

If travelling from a non-qualifying country, you will need a visitor's visa, also known as a non-immigrant visa when entering the United States for visiting friends or family, tourism or medical procedures. It is recommended that you schedule your visa interview at least 60 days before your date of travel. You will need to submit a passport that will be valid for at least 6 months after your intended travel, a birth certificate, a police certificate and color photographs that comply with US visa requirements. Proof of financial support for your stay in the United States is also required.

Health Insurance

Medical procedures are very expensive in the United States and there is no free or subsidized healthcare service. The best strategy would be to organize temporary health insurance for the duration of your stay. You will not need any special vaccinations if visiting the United States as tourists. For an immigration visa, the required immunizations are against hepatitis A and B, measles, mumps, rubella, influenza, polio, tetanus, varicella, meningococcal, pneumococcal, rotavirus, pertussis and influenza type B.

There are several companies that offer short-term health insurance packages for visitors to the United States. Coverage with Inbound USA can be purchased online through their website and offer health insurance for periods from 5 to 364 days. Visitor Secure will provide coverage for accidents and new health complications from 5 days to 2 years, but the cost and care of pre-existing medical conditions and dental care is excluded. Inbound Guest offers similar terms for periods of between 5 and 180 days and will email you a virtual membership card as soon as the contract is finalized. Physical cards will be available within one business day of arrival to the United States.

Traveling with Pets

The United States accepts EU pet passports as valid documentation for pets in transit, provided that your pet is up to date on vaccinations. In most instances, the airline you use will require a health certificate. While microchipping is not required,

PALM SPRINGS TRAVEL GUIDE

it may be helpful in case your pet gets lost. If visiting from a non-English speaking country, be sure to have an English translation of your vet's certificate available for the US authorities to examine. To be cleared for travel, your pet must have a vet's certificate issued no less than 10 days before your date of travel. Pets need to be vaccinated against rabies at least 30 days prior to entry to the United States. If the animal was recently microchipped, the microchipping procedure should have taken place prior to vaccination. In the case of dogs, it is also important that your pet must test negative for screwworm no later than 5 days before your intended arrival in the United States.

In the case of exotic pets such as parrots, turtles and other reptiles, you will need check on the CITES (Convention on International Trade in Endangered Species of Wild Fauna and Flora) status of the breed, to ensure that you will in fact be allowed to enter the United States with your pet. There are restrictions on bringing birds from certain countries and a quarantine period of 30 days also applies for birds, such as parrots. It is recommended that birds should enter the United States at New York, Los Angeles or Miami, where quarantine facilities are available. The owner of the bird will carry the expense of the quarantine and advance reservations need to be made for this, to prevent the bird being refused entry altogether. Additionally, you will need to submit documentation in the

PALM SPRINGS TRAVEL GUIDE

form of a USDA import permit as well as a health certificate issued by your veterinarian less than 30 days prior to the date of entry.

Airports

Your trip will probably be via one of the country's major gateway airports. **Hartsfield–Jackson Atlanta International Airport** (ATL), which is located less than 12km from the central business area of Atlanta in Georgia is the busiest airport in the United States and the world. It processes about 100 million passengers annually. Internationally, it offers connections to Paris, London, Frankfurt Amsterdam, Dubai, Tokyo, Mexico City and Johannesburg. Domestically, its busiest routes are to Florida, New York, Los Angeles, Dallas and Chicago. Delta Airlines maintains a huge presence at the airport, with the largest hub to be found anywhere in the world and a schedule of almost a thousand daily flights. Via a railway station, the airport provides easy access to the city.

Los Angeles International Airport (LAX) is the second busiest airport in the United States and the largest airport in the state of California. Located in the southwestern part of Los Angeles about 24km from the city center, it is easily accessibly by road and rail. Its nine passenger terminals are connected through a shuttle service. Los Angeles International Airport is a significant origin-and-destination airport for travellers to and from the United States. The second busiest airport in California is **San Francisco International Airport** (SFO) and, like Los Angeles it is an important gateway for trans-Pacific connections. It serves as an important maintenance hub for United and is home to an aviation museum. Anyone who is serious about green policies and environmentally friendly alternatives will love San Francisco's airport. There is a special bicycle route to the airport, designated bicycle parking zones and even a service that offers special freight units for travelling with your bicycle. Bicycles are also allowed on its Airtrain service. The third airport of note in California is **San Diego International Airport** (SAN).

Chicago O'Hare International Airport (ORD) is located about 27km northwest of Chicago's central business district, also known as the Chicago Loop. As a gateway to Chicago and the Great Lakes region, it is the US airport that sees the highest frequency of arrivals and departures. Terminal 5 is used for all international arrivals and most international departures, with the exception of Air Canada and some airline carriers under the Star Alliance or Oneworld brand. The Airport Transit System provides easy access for passengers between terminals and to the remote sections of the parking area.

PALM SPRINGS TRAVEL GUIDE

Located roughly halfway between the cities of Dallas and Fort Worth, **Dallas-Fort Worth International Airport** (DFW) is the primary international airport serving the state of Texas. Both in terms of passenger numbers and air traffic statistics, it ranks among the ten busiest airports in the world. It is also home to the second largest hub in the world, that of American Airlines, which is headquartered in Texas. Through 8 Interstate highways and 3 major rail services, it provides access to the city centers of both Dallas and Fort Worth, as well as the rest of Texas. An automated people mover, known as the Skylink makes it effortless for passenger to transverse between different sections of the airport and the parking areas. Terminal D is its international terminal. The second busiest airport in Texas is the **George Bush Intercontinental Airport** (IAH) in Houston, which offers connections to destinations across the United States, as well as Mexico, Canada, the Americas and selected cities in Europe and Asia.

John F. Kennedy International Airport (JFK) is located in the neighborhood of Queens. In terms of international passengers, it is one of the busiest airports in the United States, with connections to 6 continents and with the air traffic of 70 different airlines. Its busiest routes are to London, Paris, Los Angeles and San Francisco. It serves as a gateway hub for both Delta and American Airlines. Terminal 8, its newest terminal, is larger than Central Park. It has the capacity of processing

PALM SPRINGS TRAVEL GUIDE

around 1600 passengers per hour. An elevated railway service, the Airtrain provides access to all 8 of its terminals and also connects to the Long Island railroad as well as the New York City Subway in Queens. Within the airport, the service is free. Three other major airports also service the New York City area. **Newark Liberty International Airport** (EWR) is New York's second busiest airport and home of the world's third largest hub, that of United Airlines. Newark is located about 24km from Mid Manhattan, between Newark and Elizabeth. Its airtrain offers an easy way of commuting around the airport and connects via the Newark Liberty International Airport Station to the North Jersey Coast line and Northeast Corridor line. Other airports in New York are **La Guardia Airport** (LGA), located on the Flushing Bay Waterfront in Queens and **Teterboro Airport** (TEB), which is mainly used by private charter companies.

Washington D.C. is served by two airports, **Baltimore-Washington International Airport** (BWI) and **Washington Dulles International Airport** (IAD). Other important airports on the eastern side of the United States include **Logan International Airport** (BOS) in Boston, **Philadelphia International Airport** (PHL) and **Charlotte Douglas International Airport** (CLT) in North Carolina. The three busiest airports in the state of Florida are **Miami International Airport** (MIA), **Fort Lauderdale-Hollywood International**

PALM SPRINGS TRAVEL GUIDE

Airport (FLL) and **Tampa International Airport** (TPA). In the western part of the United States, **McCarran International Airport** (LAS) in Las Vegas and **Phoenix Sky Harbor International** (PHX) in Arizona offer important connections. **Denver International Airport** (DEN) in Colorado is the primary entry point to Rocky Mountains, while **Seattle-Tacoma International Airport** (SEA) in Washington State and **Portland International Airport** (PDX) in Oregon provide access to the Pacific Northwest. **Honolulu International Airport** (HNL) is the primary point of entry to Hawaii.

Airlines

The largest air carriers in the United States are United Airlines, American Airlines and Delta Airlines. Each of these could lay claim to the title of largest airline using different criteria. In terms of passenger numbers, Delta Airlines is the largest airline carrier. It was founded from humble beginnings as a crop dusting outfit in the 1920s, but grew to an enormous operation through mergers with Northeast Airlines in the 1970s, Western Airlines in the 1980s and North-western Airlines in 2010. Delta also absorbed a portion of Pan Am's assets and business, following its bankruptcy in the early 1990s. Delta Airlines operates Delta Connections, a regional service covering North American destinations in Canada, Mexico and the United

PALM SPRINGS TRAVEL GUIDE

States. In terms of destinations, United Airlines is the largest airline in the United States and the world. Its origins lie in an early airline created by Boeing in the 1920s, but the company grew from a series of acquisitions and mergers - most recently with Continental Airlines - to its current status as a leading airline. Regional services are operated under the brand United Express, in partnership with a range of feeder carriers including CapeAir, CommutAir, ExpressJet, GoJet Airlines, Mesa Airlines, Republic Airlines, Shuttle America, SkyWest Airlines and Trans State Airlines. American Airlines commands the largest fleet in the United States. It originated from the merger of over 80 tiny regional airlines in the 1930s and has subsequently merged with Trans Caribbean Airways, Air California, Reno Air, Trans World Airlines and, most recently, US Airways. Through the Oneworld Airline Alliance, American Airlines is partnered with British Airways, Finnair, Iberia and Japan Airlines. Regional connections are operated under the American Eagle brand name and include the services of Envoy Air, Piedmont Airlines, Air Wisconsin, SkyWest Airlines, Republic Airlines and PSA Airlines. American Airlines operates the American Airlines Shuttle, a service that connects the cities of New York, Boston and Washington DC with hourly flights on weekdays.

Based in Dallas, Texas, Southwest Airlines is the world's largest budget airline. It carries the highest number of domestic

PALM SPRINGS TRAVEL GUIDE

passengers in the United States and operates over 200 daily flights on its 3 busiest routes, namely Chicago, Washington and Las Vegas. JetBlue Airways is a budget airline based in Long Island that operates mainly in the Americas and the Caribbean. It covers 97 destinations in the United States, Mexico, Costa Rica, Puerto Rico, Grenada, Peru, Colombia, Bermuda, Jamaica, the Bahamas, Barbados, the Dominican Republic and Trinidad and Tobago. Spirit Airlines is an ultra low cost carrier which offers flights to destinations in the United States, Latin America, Mexico and the Caribbean. It is based in Miramar, Florida.

Alaska Airlines was founded in the 1930s to offer connections in the Pacific Northwest, but began to expand from the 1990s to include destinations east of the Rocky Mountains as well as connections to the extreme eastern part of Russia. Alaska Airlines recently acquired the brand, Virgin America which represents the Virgin brand in the United States. Silver Airways is a regional service which offers connections to various destinations in Florida, Pennsylvania, Virginia and West Virginia and provides a service to several islands within the Bahamas. Frontier Airlines is a relatively new budget airline that is mainly focussed on connections around the Rocky Mountain states. Hawaiian Airlines is based in Honolulu and offers connections to the American mainland as well as to Asia. Island Air also serves Hawaii and enjoys a partnership with

PALM SPRINGS TRAVEL GUIDE

United Airlines. Mokulele Airlines is a small airline based in Kona Island. It provides access to some of the smaller airports in the Hawaiian Islands. Sun Country Airlines is based in Minneapolis and covers destinations in the United States, Mexico, Costa Rica, Puerto Rica, Jamaica, St Maarten and the US Virgin Islands. Great Lakes Airline is a major participant in the Essential Air Service, a government programme set up to ensure that small and remote communities can be reached by air, following the deregulation of certified airlines. These regional connections include destinations in Arizona, Colorado, Kansas, Minnesota, Nebraska, New Mexico, South Dakota and Wyoming. In the past, Great Lakes Airline had covered a wide range of destinations as a partner under the United Express banner.

Hubs

Hartsfield Jackson Atlanta International Airport serves as the largest hub and headquarters of Delta Airlines. John F. Kennedy International Airport serves as a major hub for Delta's traffic to and from the European continent. Los Angeles International Airport serves as a hub for Delta Airline's connections to Mexico, Hawaii and Japan, but also serves the Florida-California route. Detroit Metropolitan Wayne County Airport is

PALM SPRINGS TRAVEL GUIDE

Delta's second largest hubs and serves as a gateway for connections to Asia.

Washington Dulles International Airport serves as a hub for United Airlines as well as Silver Airways. United Airlines also use Denver International Airport, George Bush Intercontinental Airport in Houston, Los Angeles International Airport, San Francisco International Airport, Newark Liberty International Airport and O'Hare International Airport in Chicago as hubs.

Dallas/Fort Worth International Airport serves as the primary hub for American Airlines. Its second largest hub in the southeastern part of the US is Charlotte Douglas International Airport in North Carolina and its largest hub in the north is O'Hare International Airport in Chicago. Other hubs for American Airlines are Phoenix Sky Harbor International Airport - its largest hub in the west - Miami International Airport, Ronald Reagan Washington National Airport, Los Angeles International Airport, John F Kennedy International Airport in New York, which serves as a key hub for European air traffic and La Guardia Airport also in New York.

Seattle-Tacoma International Airport serves as a primary hub for Alaska Airlines. Other hubs for Alaska include Portland International Airport, Los Angeles International Airport and Ted Stevens - Anchorage International Airport. Virgin America

PALM SPRINGS TRAVEL GUIDE

operates a primary hub at San Francisco International Airport, but also has a second hub at Los Angeles International Airport as well as a significant presence at Dallas Love Field. Denver International Airport is the primary hub for Frontier Airlines, which also has hubs at Chicago O'Hare International Airport and Orlando International Airport. Frontier also maintains a strong presence at Hartsfield-Jackson Atlanta International Airport, Cincinnati/North Kentucky International Airport, Cleveland Hopkins International Airport, McCarran International Airport in Las Vegas and Philadelphia International Airport. Honolulu International Airport and Kahului Airport serve as hubs for Hawaiian Airlines. Mokulele Airlines uses Kona International Airport and Kahului Airport as hubs. Minneapolis–Saint Paul International Airport serves as a hub for Delta Airlines, Great Lakes Airlines and Sun Country Airlines. Silver Airways uses Fort Lauderdale-Hollywood International Airport as a primary hub and also has hubs at Tampa International Airport, Orlando International Airport and Washington Dulles International Airport.

Seaports

The Port of Miami is often described as the cruise capital of the world, but it also serves as a cargo gateway to the United States. There are 8 passenger terminals and the Port Miami Tunnel, an

PALM SPRINGS TRAVEL GUIDE

undersea tunnel connects the port to the Interstate 95 via the Dolphin Expressway. Miami is an important base for several of the world's most prominent cruise lines, including Norwegian Cruise Lines, Celebrity Cruises, Royal Caribbean International and Carnival Cruises. In total, over 40 cruise ships representing 18 different cruise brands are berthed at Miami. Well over 4 million passengers are processed here annually. There are two other important ports in the state of Florida. Port Everglades is the third busiest cruise terminal in Florida, as well as its busiest cargo terminal. It is home to *Allure of the Seas* and *Oasis of the Seas*, two of the world's largest cruise ships. Oceanfront condominium dwellers often bid ships farewell with a friendly cacophony of horns and bells. The third important cruise port in Florida is Port Canaveral, which has 5 cruise terminals.

With its location on the Mississippi river, New Orleans is an important cargo port, but it also has a modern cruise terminal with over 50 check-in counters. The Port of Seattle is operated by the same organization that runs the city's airport. It has two busy cruise terminals. The Port of Los Angeles has a state of the art World Cruise Center, with three berths for passenger liners. As the oldest port on the Gulf of Mexico, the Port of Galveston dates back to the days when Texas was still part of Mexico. Galveston serves both as a cargo port and cruise terminal.

PALM SPRINGS TRAVEL GUIDE

Money Matters

Currency

The currency of the United States is US dollar (USD). Notes are issued in denominations of $1, $2, $5, $10, $20, $50 and $100. Coins are issued in denominations of $1 (known as a silver dollar, 50c (known as a half dollar), 25c (quarter), 10c (dime), 5c (nickel) and 1c (penny).

Banking/ATMs

ATM machines are widely distributed across the United States and are compatible with major networks such as Cirrus and Plus for international bank transactions. Most debit cards will display a Visa or MasterCard affiliation, which means that you may be able to use them as a credit card as well. A transaction fee will be charged for withdrawals, but customers of certain bank groups such as Deutsche Bank and Barclays, can be charged smaller transaction fees or none at all, when using the ATM machines of Bank of America. While banking hours will vary, depending on the location and banking group, you can generally expect most banks to be open between 8.30am and 5pm. You will be asked for ID in the form of a passport, when using your debit card for over-the-counter transactions.

PALM SPRINGS TRAVEL GUIDE

While you cannot open a bank account in the United States without a social security number, you may want to consider obtaining a pre-paid debit card, where a fixed amount can be pre-loaded. This service is available from various credit card companies in the United States. The American Express card is called Serve and can be used with a mobile app. You can load more cash at outlets of Walmart, CVS Pharmacy, Dollar General, Family Dollar, Rite Aid and participating 7/Eleven stores.

🌎 Credit Cards

Credit cards are widely used in the United States and the the major cards - MasterCard, Visa, American Express and Diners Club – are commonly accepted. A credit card is essential in paying for hotel accommodation or car rental. As a visitor, you may want to check about the fees levied on your card for foreign exchange transactions. While Europe and the UK have already converted to chip-and-pin credit card, the transition is still in progress in the United States. Efforts are being made to make the credit cards of most US stores compliant with chip-and-pin technology. You may find that many stores still employ the older protocols at point-of-sales. Be sure to inform your bank or credit card vendor of your travel plans before leaving home.

🌐 Tourist Tax

In the United States, tourist tax varies from city to city, and can be charged not only on accommodation, but also restaurant bills, car rental and other services that cater mainly to tourists. In 22 states, some form of state wide tax is charged for accommodation and 38 states levy a tax on car rental. The city that levies the highest tax bill is Chicago. Apart from a flat fee of $2.75, you can expect to be charged 16 percent per day on hotel accommodation as well as nearly 25% for car rentals. New York charges an 18 percent hotel tax, as does Nashville, while Kansas City, Houston and Indianapolis levy around 17 percent per day hotel tax. Expect to pay 16.5 percent tax per day on your hotel bill in Cleveland and 15.6 percent per day in Seattle, with a 2 percent hike, if staying in the Seattle Tourism Improvement Area. Las Vegas charges 12 percent hotel tax. In Los Angeles, you will be charged a whopping 14 percent on your hotel room, but in Burbank, California, the rate is only 2 percent. Dallas, Texas only charges 2 percent on hotels with more than a hundred rooms. In Portland a city tax of 6 percent is added to a county tax of 5.5 percent. Do inquire about the hotel tax rate in the city where you intend to stay, when booking your accommodation.

🌐 Sales Tax

In the United States, the sales tax rate is set at state level, but in most states local counties can set an additional surtax. In some states, groceries and/or prescription drugs will be exempt from tax or charged at a lower rate. There are only five states that charge no state sales tax at all. They are Oregon, Delaware, New Hampshire, Alaska and Montana. Alaska allows a local tax rate not exceeding 7 percent and in Montana, local authorities are enabled to set a surtax rate, should they wish to do so. The state sales tax is generally set at between 4 percent (Alabama, Georgia, Louisiana, and Wyoming) and 7 percent (Indiana, Mississippi, New Jersey, Tennessee, Rhode Island) although there are exceptions outside that spectrum with Colorado at 2.8 percent and California at 7.5 percent. The local surcharge can be anything from 4.7 percent (Hawaii) to around 11 percent (Oklahoma and Louisiana). Can you claim back tax on your US purchases as a tourist? In the United States, sales tax is added retro-actively upon payment, which means that it will not be included in the marked price of the goods you buy. Because it is set at state, rather than federal level, it is usually

PALM SPRINGS TRAVEL GUIDE

not refundable.

Two states do offer sales tax refunds to tourists. In Texas you will be able to get tax back from over 6000 participating stores if the tax amount came to more than $12 and the goods were purchased within 30 days of your departure. To qualify, you need to submit the original sales receipts, your passport, flight or transport information and visa details. Refunds are made in cash, cheque or via PayPal. Louisiana was the first state to introduce tax refunds for tourists. To qualify there, you must submit all sales receipts, together with your passport and flight ticket at a Refund Center outlet.

Tipping

Tipping is very common in the United States. In sit-down restaurants, a tip of between 10 and 15 percent of the bill is customary. At many restaurants, the salaries of waiting staff will be well below minimum wage levels. With large groups of diners, the restaurant may charge a mandatory gratuity, which is automatically included in the bill. At the trendiest New York restaurants, a tip of 25 percent may be expected. While you can add a credit card tip, the best way to ensure the gratuity reaches your server is to tip separately in cash. Although tipping is less of an obligation at takeaway restaurants, such as McDonalds,

PALM SPRINGS TRAVEL GUIDE

you can leave your change, or otherwise $1, if there is a tip jar on the counter. In the case of pizza delivery, a minimum of $3 is recommended and more is obviously appreciated. Although a delivery charge is often levied, this money usually goes to the pizzeria, rather than the driver. Tip a taxi driver 10 percent of the total fare. At your hotel, tip the porter between $1 and $2 per bag. Tip between 10 and 20 percent at hair salons, spas, beauty salons and barber shops. Tip tour guides between 10 and 20 percent for a short excursion. For a day trip, tip both the guide and the driver $5 to $10 per person, if a gratuity is not included in the cost of the tour. Tip the drivers of charter or sightseeing buses around $1 per person.

Connectivity

Mobile Phones

There are four major service providers for wireless connection in the United States. They are Verizon Wireless, T-Mobile US, AT&T Mobility and Sprint. Not all are compatible with European standards. While most countries in Europe, Asia, the Middle East and East Africa uses the GSM mobile network, only two US service providers, T-Mobile and AT&T Mobility aligns with this. Also bear in mind that GSM carriers in the United States operate using the 850 MHz/1900 MHz frequency

PALM SPRINGS TRAVEL GUIDE

bands, whereas the UK, all of Europe, Asia, Australia and Africa use 900/1800MHz. You should check with your phone's tech specifications to find out whether it supports these standards. The other services, Verizon Wireless and Sprint use the CDMA network standard and, while Verizon's LTE frequencies are somewhat compatible with those of T-Mobile and AT&T, Sprint uses a different bandwidth for its LTE coverage.

To use your own phone, you can purchase a T-Mobile 3-in-1 starter kit for $20. If your device is unlocked, GMS-capable and supports either Band II (1900 MHz) or Band IV (1700/2100 MHz), you will be able to access the T-Mobile network. You can also purchase an AT&T sim card through the Go Phone Pay-as-you-go plan for as little as $0.99. Refill cards are available from $25 and are valid for 90 days. If you want to widen your network options, you may want to explore the market for a throwaway or disposable phone. At Walmart, you can buy non-contracted phones for as little as $9.99, as well as pre-paid sim cards and data top-up packages.

Canadians travellers will find the switch to US networks technically effortless, but should watch out for roaming costs. Several American networks do offer special international rates for calls to Canada or Mexico.

PALM SPRINGS TRAVEL GUIDE

☻ Dialing Code

The international dialing code for the United States is +1.

☻ Emergency Numbers

General Emergency: 911 (this number can be used free of charge from any public phone in the United States).
MasterCard: 1-800-307-7309
Visa: 1-800-847-2911

☻ General Information

☻ Public Holidays

1 January: New Year's Day
3rd Monday in January: Martin Luther King Day
3rd Monday in February: President's Day
Last Monday in May: Memorial Day
4 July: Independence Day
1st Monday in September: Labour Day
2nd Monday in October: Columbus Day
11 November: Veteran's Day
4th Thursday in November: Thanksgiving Day

PALM SPRINGS TRAVEL GUIDE

4th Friday in November: Day after Thanksgiving

25 December: Christmas Day (if Christmas Day falls on a Sunday, the Monday thereafter is a public holiday.) In some states, 26 December is a public holiday as well.

There are several festivals that are not public holidays per se, but are culturally observed in the United States. They include:

14 February: Valentine's Day

17 March: St Patrick's Day

March/April (variable): Easter or Passover

Second Sunday in May: Mother's Day

3rd Sunday in June: Father's Day

31 October: Halloween

Time Zones

The United States has 6 different time zones. **Eastern Standard Time** is observed in the states of Maine, New York, New Hampshire, Delaware, Vermont, Maryland, Rhode Island, Massachusetts, Connecticut, Pennsylvania, Ohio, North Carolina, South Carolina, Georgia, Virginia, West Virginia, Michigan, most of Florida and Indiana as well as the eastern parts of Kentucky and Tennessee. Eastern Standard Time is calculated as Greenwich Meantime/Coordinated Universal Time (UTC) -5. **Central Standard Time** is observed in Iowa, Illinois, Missouri, Arkansas, Louisiana, Oklahoma, Kansas,

PALM SPRINGS TRAVEL GUIDE

Mississippi, Alabama, near all of Texas, the western half of Kentucky, the central and western part of Tennessee, sections of the north-western and south-western part of Indiana, most of North and South Dakota, the eastern and central part of Nebraska and the north-western strip of Florida, also known as the Florida Panhandle. Central Standard Time is calculated as Greenwich Meantime/Coordinated Universal Time (UTC) -6. **Mountain Standard Time** is observed in New Mexico, Colorado, Wyoming, Montana, Utah, Arizona, the southern and central section of Idaho, the western parts of Nebraska, South Dakota and North Dakota, a portion of eastern Oregon and the counties of El Paso and Hudspeth in Texas. Mountain Standard Time is calculated as Greenwich Meantime/Coordinated Universal Time (UTC) -7. **Pacific Standard Time** is used in California, Washington, Nevada, most of Oregon and the northern part of Idaho. Pacific Standard Time is calculated as Greenwich Meantime/Coordinated Universal Time (UTC) -8. **Alaska Standard Time** is used in Alaska and this can be calculated as Greenwich Meantime/Coordinated Universal Time (UTC) -9. Because of its distant location, Hawaii is in a time zone of its own. **Hawaii Standard Time** can be calculated as Greenwich Meantime/Coordinated Universal Time (UTC) -10.

PALM SPRINGS TRAVEL GUIDE

🌎 Daylight Savings Time

Clocks are set forward one hour at 2.00am on the second Sunday of March and set back one hour at 2.00am on the first Sunday of November for Daylight Savings Time. The states of Hawaii and Arizona do not observe Daylight Savings Time. However, the Navajo Indian Reservation, which extends across three states (Arizona, Utah and New Mexico), does observe Daylight Savings Time throughout its lands, including that portion which falls within Arizona.

🌎 School Holidays

In the United States, the academic year begins in September, usually in the week just before or after Labour Day and ends in the early or middle part of June. There is a Winter Break that includes Christmas and New Year and a Spring Break in March or April that coincides with Easter. In some states, there is also a Winter Break in February. The summer break occurs in the 10 to 11 weeks between the ending of one academic year and the commencement of the next academic year. Holidays may vary according to state and certain weather conditions such as hurricanes or snowfall may also lead to temporary school closures in affected areas.

PALM SPRINGS TRAVEL GUIDE

🌐 Trading Hours

Trading hours in the United States vary. Large superstores like Walmart trade round the clock at many of its outlets, or else between 7am and 10pm. Kmart is often open from 8am to 10pm, 7 days a week. Target generally opens at 8am and may close at 10 or 11pm, depending on the area. Many malls will open at 10am and close at 9pm. Expect restaurants to be open from about 11am to 10pm or 11pm, although the hours of eateries that serve alcohol and bars may be restricted by local legislation. Banking hours also vary, according to branch and area. Branches of the Bank of America will generally open at 9am, and closing time can be anywhere between 4pm and 6pm. Most post office outlets are open from 9am to 5pm on weekdays.

🌐 Driving

In the United States, motorists drive on the right hand side of the road. As public transport options are not always adequate, having access to a car is virtually essential, when visiting the United States. To drive, you will need a valid driver's licence from your own country, in addition to an international driving permit. If your driver's licence does not include a photograph,

PALM SPRINGS TRAVEL GUIDE

you will be asked to submit your passport for identification as well.

For car rental, you will also need a credit card. Some companies do not rent out vehicles to drivers under the age of 25. Visitors with a UK license may need to obtain a check code for rental companies, should they wish to verify the details and validity of their driver's licence, via the DVLA view-your-licence service. This can also be generated online, but must be done at least 72 hours prior to renting the car. In most cases, though, the photo card type license will be enough. The largest rental companies - Alamo, Avis, Budget, Hertz, Dollar and Thrifty - are well represented in most major cities and usually have offices at international airports. Do check about the extent of cover included in your travel insurance package and credit card agreement. Some credit card companies may include Collision Damage Waiver (CDW), which will cover you against being held accountable for any damage to the rental car, but it is recommended that you also arrange for personal accident insurance, out-of-state insurance and supplementary liability insurance. You can sometimes cut costs on car rentals by reserving a car via the internet before leaving home.

The maximum speed limit in the United States varies according to state, but is usually between 100km per hour (65 m.p.h.) and 120km per hour (75 m.p.h.). For most of the Eastern states, as

PALM SPRINGS TRAVEL GUIDE

well as California and Oregon on the west coast the maximum speed driven on interstate highways should be 110km per hour (70 m.p.h.). Urban speed legislation varies, but in business and residential areas, speeds are usually set between 32km (20 miles) and 48km (30 miles) per hour. In Colorado, nighttime speed limits apply in certain areas where migrating wildlife could be endangered and on narrow, winding mountain passes, a limit of 32km (20 miles) per hour sometimes applies. In most American states there is a ban on texting for all drivers and a ban on all cell phone use for novice drivers.

Drinking

It is illegal in all 50 states for persons under the age of 21 to purchase alcohol or to be intoxicated. In certain states, such as Texas, persons between the age of 18 and 21 may be allowed to drink beer or wine, if in the company of a parent or legal guardian. In most states, the trading hours for establishments selling alcohol is limited. There are a few exceptions to this. In Nevada, alcohol may be sold round the clock and with few restrictions other than age. In Louisiana, there are no restrictions on trading in alcohol at state level, although some counties set their own restrictions. By contrast, Arizona has some of the strictest laws in relation to alcohol sales, consumption and driving under the influence. The sale of alcohol is prohibited on Native American reservations, unless

PALM SPRINGS TRAVEL GUIDE

the tribal council of that reservation has passed a vote to lift restrictions.

🌐 Smoking

There is no smoking ban set at federal level in the United States. At state level, there are 40 states in total that enact some form of state wide restriction on smoking, although the exemptions of individual states may vary. In Arizona, California, Colorado, Connecticut, Delaware, Hawaii, Illinois, Iowa, Kansas, Maine, Maryland, Massachusetts, Michigan, Minnesota, Montana, Nebraska, North Dakota, New Jersey, New Mexico, New York, Ohio, Oregon, Rhode Island, South Dakota, Utah, Vermont, Washington and Wisconsin, smoking is prohibited in all public enclosed areas, including bars and restaurants. The states of Arkansas, Florida, Indiana, Louisiana, Pennsylvania and Tennessee do have a general state wide restriction on smoking in public places, but exempt adult venues where under 21s are not allowed. This includes bars, restaurants, betting shops and gaming parlours (Indiana) and casinos (Louisiana and Pennsylvania). Nevada also has a state wide ban on smoking that exempts casinos, bars, strip clubs and brothels. In Georgia, state wide smoking legislation exempts bars and restaurants that only serve patrons over the age of 18. Idaho has a state wide ban that includes restaurants, but

PALM SPRINGS TRAVEL GUIDE

exempts bars serving only alcohol. New Hampshire, North Carolina and Virginia have also introduced some form of state wide smoking restriction. While the states of Alabama, Alaska, Kentucky, Mississippi, Missouri, Oklahoma, South Carolina, Texas, West Virginia and Wyoming have no state legislation, there are more specific restrictions at city and county level. In Arizona, there is an exemption for businesses located on Native American reservation and, in particular, for Native American religious ceremonies that may include smoking rituals. In California, the first state to implement anti-smoking legislation, smoking is also prohibited in parks and on sidewalks.

Electricity

Electricity: 110 volts

Frequency: 60 Hz

Electricity sockets are compatible with American Type A and Type B plugs. The Type A plug features two flat prongs or blades, while the Type B plug has the same plus an additional 'earth' prong. Most newer models of camcorders and cameras are dual voltage, which means that you should be able to charge them without an adapter in the United States, as they have a built in converter for voltage. You may find that appliances from the UK or Europe which were designed to accommodate a higher voltage will not function as effectively in the United

States. While a current converter or transformer will be able to adjust the voltage, you may still experience some difficulty with the type of devices that are sensitive to variations in frequency as the United States uses 60 Hz, instead of the 50 Hz which is common in Europe and the UK. Appliances like hairdryers will usually be available in hotels and since electronic goods are fairly cheap in the United States, the easiest strategy may be to simply purchase a replacement. Bear in mind, that you may need an adaptor or transformer to operate it once you return home.

🌐 Food & Drink

Hamburgers, hot dogs and apple pie may be food items that come to mind when considering US culinary stereotypes, but Americans eat a wide variety of foods. They love steaks and ribs when dining out and pancakes or waffles for breakfast. As a society which embraces various immigrant communities, America excels at adopting and adapting traditional staples and adding its own touch to them. Several "Asian" favorites really originated in the United States. These include the California roll (offered in sushi restaurants) and the fortune cookie (chinese). Popular Hispanic imports include tacos, enchiladas and burritos. Another stereotype of American cuisine is large portion sizes. Hence the existence of American inventions such as the

PALM SPRINGS TRAVEL GUIDE

footlong sub, the footlong chilli cheese hot dog and the Krispy Creme burger, which combines a regular hamburger with a donut. Corn dogs are fairground favorites. Most menus are more balanced however. It is common to ask for a doggy bag (to take away remaining food) in a restaurant.

When in the South, enjoy corn bread, grits and southern fried chicken. Try spicy buffalo wings in New York, traditionally prepared baked beans in Boston and deep dish pizza in Chicago. French fries are favorites with kids of all ages, but Americans also love their potatoes as hash browns or the bite sized tater tots. Indulge your sweet tooth with Twinkies, pop tarts, cup cakes and banana splits. Popular sandwiches include the BLT (bacon, lettuce, tomato, the Reuben sandwich, the sloppy joe and the peanut butter and jelly.

Sodas (fizzy drinks) and bottled waters are the top beverages in the United States. The top selling soft drinks are Coca Cola, followed by Pepsi Cola, Diet Coke, Mountain Dew and Dr Pepper. In America's colonial past, tea was initially the hot beverage of choice and it was tea politics that kicked off the American Revolution, but gradually tea has been replaced by coffee in popularity. From the 1970s, Starbucks popularized coffee culture in the United States. Americans still drink gallons of tea and they are particularly fond of a refreshing glass of iced tea. Generally, Americans drink more beer than wine and favorite brands include Bud Light, followed by Coors Light, Budweiser and Miller Light. Popular cocktails are the Martini, the Manhattan, the Margarita, the Bloody Mary, the Long Island Ice tea and Sex on the Beach.

American Sports

Baseball is widely regarded as the national sport of America. The sport originated in the mid 1800s and superficially shares the basic objective of cricket, which is to score runs by hitting a ball pitched by the opposing team, but in baseball, the innings ends as soon as three players have been caught out. A point is scored when a runner has passed three bases and reached the 4th or home base of the baseball diamond. After 9 innings, the team with the highest number of runs is declared the winner. The Baseball World Series is played in the fall (autumn), usually in October, and consists of best-of-seven play-off between the two top teams representing the rival affiliations of the National League and American League.

Although the origins of American football can be found in rugby, the sport is now widely differentiated from its roots and today numerous distinctions exist between the two. In American football, a game is divided into four quarters, with each team fielding 11 players, although unlimited substitution is allowed.

PALM SPRINGS TRAVEL GUIDE

Players wear helmets and heavy padding as any player can be tackled, regardless of ball possession. An annual highlight is the Super Bowl, the championship game of the National Football League. The event is televised live to over a 100 million viewers and features a high profile halftime performance by a top music act. Super bowl Sunday traditionally takes place on the first Sunday of February.

The roots of stock car racing can be found in America's prohibition era, when bootleggers needed powerful muscle cars (often with modifications for greater speed) to transport their illicit alcohol stocks. Informal racing evolved to a lively racing scene in Daytona, Florida. An official body, NASCAR, was founded in 1948 to regulate the sport, NASCAR. Today, NASCAR racing has millions of fans. One of its most prestigious events is the Sprint Cup, a championship which comprises of 36 races and kicks off each year with the Daytona 500.

Rodeo originated from the chores and day-to-day activities of Spanish cattle farmers and later, the American ranchers who occupied the former Spanish states such as Texas, California and Arizona. The advent of fencing eliminated the need for cattle drives, but former cowboys found that their skills still offered good entertainment, providing a basis for wild west shows such as those presented by Buffalo Bill. Soon, rodeo

PALM SPRINGS TRAVEL GUIDE

events became the highlight of frontier towns throughout the west. During the first half of the 20th centuries, organizations formed to regulate events. Today, rodeo is considered a legitimate national sport with millions of fans. If you want to experience the thrill of this extreme sport, attend one of its top events. The Prescott Frontier Days show in Arizona is billed to be America's oldest rodeo. The Reno Rodeo in Nevada is a 10 day event that takes place in mid-June and includes the option of closer participation as a volunteer. Rodeo Houston, a large 20 day event that takes place towards the end of winter, is coupled to a livestock show. Visit the San Antonio show in Texas during February for the sheer variety of events. The National Western Rodeo in Denver Colorado is an indoor event that attracts up to half a million spectators each year. The National Finals that takes place in Las Vegas during December is the prestigious championship that marks the end of the year's rodeo calendar.

Useful Websites

https://esta.cbp.dhs.gov/esta/ -- The US Electronic System for Travel Authorization
http://www.visittheusa.com/
http://roadtripusa.com/
http://www.roadtripamerica.com/

PALM SPRINGS TRAVEL GUIDE

http://www.road-trip-usa.info/

http://www.autotoursusa.com/

http://www.onlyinyourstate.com/

http://www.theamericanroadtripcompany.co.uk/

Manufactured by Amazon.ca
Bolton, ON